Prohibited!

Written by John Parsons

NELSON

THOMSON LEARNING

Chapter Snapshots

"Make your decision ..."

A Guide To Web Design

In this book, *Prohibited!*, you will find that all of the following pages are designed to look like a web page that you might find on the Internet. People or organisations that design web pages for Internet sites try to present information in a way that is interesting, easy to read and easy to understand. They use different types of graphics to help you decide where you want to go in their website.

In most web pages, you can click on coloured text for more information. You might also be able to click on different buttons to take you to another part of the website or to make a decision about something you have read in the website. The website will also tell you how many pages it has, and what page number you are up to.

The following chapters present a number of facts and opinions that you must use to make a decision on each important conservation issue. When you have read all the information, it is up to you to decide what to do!

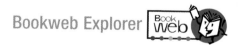

1. Whaling

Bookweb Explorer    GO

Good morning! Along with other citizens, you have the opportunity to make some important decisions on four environmental issues. Your job, should you choose to accept it, will be to examine the background to each issue and make a final choice. Please follow the screens below to enable you to make your choice on each issue.

ISSUE — SHOULD WE COMPLETELY BAN **WHALING**?

ANIMAL — MANY DIFFERENT SPECIES OF **WHALES**

LOCATION — PACIFIC, ATLANTIC and ARCTIC OCEANS

Reason For Exploitation

Since the 1500s, whales have been hunted to provide many products for human use. As well as meat, whales provided oil for lighting and making margarine and soap, wax for making candles, ambergris for making perfume, organs for making medicines, and bones for strengthening clothes and making umbrellas. Almost every part of the whale was valuable and could be used for something.

This illustration from the 1500s shows Spanish whalers cutting up a whale.

Recent Changes

Towards the end of the 1800s, the value of whale oil and wax had dropped. New fuels, such as petroleum and oil, had been discovered and were much cheaper to produce. By the 1920s, newly invented plastics were taking the place of whale bone in clothes and umbrellas. Very few whale products could not be made by other means. Only the meat and internal organs were in demand.

Whale Bones

Whale bones were used to strengthen corsets. Corsets were worn by women to squeeze their upper body into a thinner shape. By the 1920s, newly invented plastics replaced whale bone. By the 1950s, it was no longer fashionable to wear tight corsets.

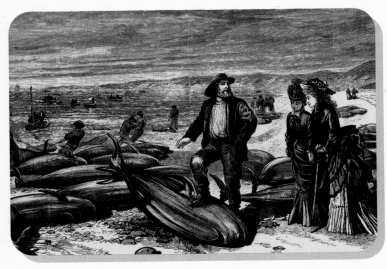

In 1946, the countries that permitted whaling formed a group to agree on reducing the numbers of whales they would hunt. In 1982, the group, called the International Whaling Commission, decided to stop all whaling. Whales were becoming extremely rare, due to too much hunting. Many people also believed that whales were very intelligent, and that whaling was cruel. Some people, however, disagreed and carried on whaling. Despite protests, many whales are still killed each year.

Summary Of Arguments For Banning Whaling

1. Whales are endangered.

2. Other materials can easily and cheaply replace whale products.

3. Whales may be intelligent and hunting them is cruel.

Arguments Against Completely Banning Whaling

Please read the following e-mail:

Dear Decision-maker:

We represent a group of people in Japan, Norway, Iceland and the Arctic. We are against a complete ban on whaling for the following reasons.

1. Some native people, such as the Inuit of North America, rely on the meat and blubber from whales to eat. They also use the bones for building, tools and making fishing nets. As they use only small boats and traditional weapons, such as spears, to catch a small number of whales each year, they do not endanger the total whale population.

2. We believe it is important that people who work for the whaling industry in Japan, Norway and Iceland are allowed to keep their jobs. If they were not allowed to hunt whales, many people who work as whalers would find it difficult to find other kinds of work. This will cause problems for them, their families and their communities.

3. Some people like to eat whale meat. Because it is so expensive, whale meat is saved for special occasions. We think that if people want to eat whale meat, they should be allowed to. It is not fair to tell people what they can or cannot eat.

As long as we do not kill all the whales, we think we should be allowed to hunt them.

Yours faithfully,
Concerned Whalers
Group

You now have all the information required to make your decision. Remember, you must think about all the **facts** and **opinions** that you have read, and decide which ones you think are important. Once you have made your decision, you cannot change your mind. When you are ready, **make your choice**. Please proceed carefully.

ISSUE — SHOULD WE COMPLETELY BAN **WHALING?**

AGREE Click One **DISAGREE**

Back
 Forward
 Stop
 Refresh
 Home
 File
 Search
 Text
 Mail
 Online

2. Ivory Trading

  GO

Thank you for your decision on whaling. Your choice has been recorded, the Concerned Whalers Group will be informed, and action will be taken. You are now ready to familiarise yourself with facts and opinions about the second environmental issue. Please read the screens below to enable you to make your choice on another important issue.

ISSUE — SHOULD **IVORY TRADING** BE ALLOWED?

ANIMALS — **ELEPHANTS** and **RHINOCEROSES**

LOCATION — AFRICA, INDIA and **MIDDLE EAST**

Reason For Exploitation

Elephant tusks are made up of ivory, a hard, white substance that is highly valued. Ivory, which was once used to make piano keys, can also be carved into beautiful jewellery, small statues, and special buttons for Japanese kimonos.

Rhinoceros horns are even more valuable than ivory. But unlike tusks, which are really teeth, the horn of a rhino is made up of a hair-like substance. The horns are ground up and used as medicines in Asia. They are also used as handles on special knives in parts of the Middle East.

Recent Changes

In the twentieth century, the number of elephants declined from two million to 600,000. In the last 25 years, the number of wild black rhinoceroses have fallen from 30,000 to 3,000. These declines have been caused by hunting, and a loss of their habitat due to the spread of farming. Killing elephants and rhinoceroses for their tusks and horns is now illegal in most countries. Kenya, which is home to many of Africa's elephants, banned the ivory trade in 1989.

Even though people who hunt these animals face tough penalties, some people are tempted by the huge amounts of money they can make by selling ivory and rhinoceros horn. These people are called poachers.

Poachers sell their ivory and rhino horns to people in China. In this country, ivory is still popular. It can be sold for more money than the same weight of gold!

Reserves where elephants and rhinoceroses can live safely have been created in Africa. Wildlife police and reserve wardens work to keep poachers out of the reserves. Local people can make money from tourists who want to see elephants and rhinoceroses in their natural environment.

People who want something that looks like ivory, can use vegetable ivory. Vegetable ivory is made in Colombia from the seeds of palm trees. It can be carved, made into buttons, and into cheaper jewellery.

Summary Of Arguments Against Ivory Trading

1. Elephants and rhinoceroses are endangered.

2. Other materials can easily and cheaply replace ivory products.

3. Money can be made from tourists who want to see live animals.

Back   Forward   Stop   Refresh   Home   File   Search   Text   Mail   Online

Ivory: 123456

Bookweb Explorer  () GO

Arguments For Ivory Trading

Please read the following e-mail:

Dear Decision-maker:

   I represent a group of villagers in a remote area of Africa. We want to be allowed to trade ivory for the following reasons.

   1. No tourists come here, because it is too far to travel. We are very poor. There is no work, and it is difficult to grow enough food to eat. But we need to support our families and our communities, or they will be hungry and homeless. We can sell the tusks from just one elephant for more money than most of us could make in a year. That will let us feed, clothe and shelter our families. There are hundreds of elephants left in our area — but I only have one family. Is it fair that they should go hungry to save one elephant a year?

   2. If the ivory trade is stopped, the price of the ivory will go up. This will mean that people will want even more ivory to make more money. If we allow a small amount of ivory to be traded, we might save elephants that greedy poachers might hunt instead.

   3. Some cultures, such as those in China and Yemen, believe that rhinoceros horns have special powers. They believe that the medicines they make from rhinoceros horns help to cure sicknesses. The knives they make from rhinoceros horns are also special in some cultures. Just because your culture does not believe these things, is it fair to stop our culture using them in the ways we have for thousands of years?

   Because ivory and rhinoceros horns are so valuable, we would be irresponsible to kill all these precious animals. We would be better off being allowed to kill only as many as we need — just like you kill as many cattle, sheep, chickens and pigs as you need.

Yours faithfully,
Concerned Villagers Association

You now have all the information required to make your decision. Remember, you must think about all the **facts** and **opinions** that you have read, and decide which ones you think are important. Once you have made your decision, you cannot change your mind. When you are ready, **make your choice**. Please proceed carefully.

ISSUE SHOULD **IVORY TRADING** BE ALLOWED?

AGREE Click One DISAGREE

Back

Forward

Stop

Refresh

Home

File

Search

AA
Text

Mail

Online

Extra Facts: 1

Bookweb Explorer   GO

Moby Dick

Herman Melville was born in New York in 1819. At first, he worked in a hat shop and as a bank clerk, but he wanted to find a job with more adventure. In 1841, he joined a whaling ship crew bound for the Pacific Ocean.

In 1851, after many adventures, Melville returned to New York. There, he wrote *Moby Dick*, a classic novel about a sea captain hunting a great white whale. Unfortunately for Melville, people didn't like his book, and he had to work as a customs inspector to make a living. It was only after he died in 1891 that people began to appreciate Melville's book.

Animal Horns

People have always regarded animal horns as having special powers. The unicorn was a legendary horse-like animal whose single horn was supposed to possess magical powers. Although there is no evidence unicorns ever existed, people in the Middle Ages paid enormous sums of money for what they thought were 'unicorn horns'. It now seems likely these horns were actually the tusks of walruses or a kind of whale called a narwhale.

3. Seal Hunting

Thank you for your decision on the ivory trade. Your choice has been recorded, the Concerned Villagers Association will be informed, and action will be taken. You are now ready for familiarisation on the third environmental issue. Please follow the screens below to enable you to make your choice on the next important issue.

ISSUE — SHOULD **SEAL HUNTING** BE ALLOWED?

ANIMAL — ADULT AND CUB **SEALS**

LOCATION — **ATLANTIC**, **PACIFIC** and **ARCTIC OCEANS**

Reason For Exploitation

For hundreds of years, seals were hunted by sealers in Europe, North America, Australia and New Zealand. Like whales, seals have a thick coating of fat, called blubber, to keep themselves warm. Valuable oils, for heating and lighting, could be made from their blubber. Seal meat, too, was popular in some countries. But the most valuable part of a seal was its fur.

Back

Forward

Stop

Refresh

Home

File

Search

Text

Mail

Online

Seals: 12**3**456

Bookweb Explorer   GO

In the cold climates of northern Europe and North America, fur coats provided people with the best protection from the weather. Seal fur was the most highly prized, because it was soft and warm. The most valuable kind of fur came from the young pup of the harp seal. When it is very young, the harp seal pup has soft, white fur that was also ideal for luxury clothing.

Recent Changes

In the second half of the twentieth century, seals became extremely rare in many parts of the world. Because they were so easy to catch, many populations simply disappeared after years of hunting. As the most expensive furs came from young seals, many seals did not get a chance to grow into adults and have their own pups. This further reduced the numbers of seals.

Seals: 123<u>4</u>56

Bookweb Explorer   ( ) **GO**

When synthetic fabrics became available, the need for real fur to make warm clothing disappeared. Using animal furs to make fashionable clothes became unpopular, as people thought it was cruel to kill animals when synthetic fur was available. Sealing was banned in some countries.

In the 1970s, many people were horrified when they saw TV pictures of seal hunting in Canada. Protesters tried to stop the seal hunting by spraying the furs of the young seals with dye. This dye made their furs worthless for clothing. Still, many thousands of young seals were killed. Sealing is still allowed in parts of Canada and in some other countries in the Arctic region.

Summary Of Arguments Against Seal Hunting

1. Many types of seals are endangered.

2. Killing seals for fashionable clothes is cruel and unnecessary.

3. Killing baby seals means less adult seals in future years.

Back	Forward	Stop	Refresh	Home	File	Search	Text	Mail	Online

Seals: 123456

Bookweb Explorer **( ) GO**

Arguments For Allowing Seal Hunting

Please read the following e-mail:

Dear Decision-maker:

I represent a group of Arctic sealers. We hope you will allow us to keep sealing for the following reasons.

1. We come from communities that rely on the sea for food and clothing. When sealing stops, the numbers of seals in an area increases rapidly, and they eat a lot of the fish. When the seals eat too many fish, we cannot catch enough to make a living.

2. Once the seals in an area have eaten most of the fish, they face problems, too. Seals become malnourished, many become ill, and some may starve. We do not think that dying of starvation is any kinder than being killed quickly by a seal hunter. Do you?

3. We live in remote parts of the world, where there is no other work. Sealing is not pleasant work, and no-one enjoys it. But it is the only work we have. Without our jobs, we don't know what we will do.

We believe there are parts of the world where there are plenty of seals, and therefore we should be allowed to hunt them. We know that many people don't like to see pictures of seals being killed, and think that the pups are cute and cuddly. We think that lambs, calves and chickens are cute and cuddly, too. Why can those cute animals be used for food and clothing (yes, clothing — that's where leather comes from), but we can't use seals?

Yours faithfully,
Concerned Sealers Group

Seals: 123456

You now have all the information required to make your decision. Remember, you must think about all the **facts** and **opinions** that you have read, and decide which ones you think are important. Once you have made your decision, you cannot change your mind. When you are ready, **make your choice**. Please proceed carefully.

ISSUE   SHOULD **SEAL HUNTING** BE ALLOWED?

AGREE   Click One   **DISAGREE**

Extra Facts: 2

Inuit Seal Hunting Technology

Native North Americans, or Inuit, relied upon seals for food, clothing, warmth and tools. They used different technology to catch seals at different times of the year. In winter, when thick ice covered the Arctic Ocean, they waited at the holes in the ice that seals used to breathe. Because the holes might be very deep, the Inuit made rods of feathers and bone to put in the holes as a 'seal indicator'. When a seal surfaced inside the hole, their presence would cause the rods to shake. The Inuit would know to strike at that moment.

Inuit used long harpoons made of bone or ivory. A short, strong cord made of sealskin would be tied to the harpoon head and, once a seal had been harpooned, the Inuit hunter would hold onto the cord as the seal dived underwater. Eventually, the seal would tire, and it

could be pulled up through the breathing hole.

During summer, when seals could be hunted from the edge of an ice sheet or from boats, an inflatable sealskin was added to the line. This would slow the seal down, and help the Inuit keep track of where it was. Sometimes, seals were hunted on the ice. Inuit used movable hunting screens to hide behind while stalking seals on the ice.

4. Tiger Hunting

 GO

Thank you for your decision on seal hunting. Your choice has been recorded, the Concerned Sealers Group will be informed, and action will be taken. You are now ready to familiarise yourself on the fourth environmental issue. Please follow the screens below to enable you to make your decision on this important issue.

ISSUE — SHOULD **TIGER HUNTING** BE ALLOWED?

ANIMAL — **TIGERS**

LOCATION — **INDIA** and **ASIA**

Reason For Exploitation

Once, tiger hunting was thought to be a great sport. A hundred years ago, over 100,000 tigers lived in India. Tiger hunting has reduced the number of tigers to only 5,000 at present. Tiger skins were thought to be fine trophies, and many people had tiger skins proudly displayed on their walls.

Parts of the tiger were also used to fight illnesses by the Chinese. Chinese doctors used the internal organs and bones of the tiger in their traditional medicines.

As the human population in India and Asia grew larger, more and more land was needed for farmers to grow food. Farmers hunted tigers to stop them killing their animals. But as more land was needed for farming, the tigers were not able to find enough of their natural food. Unfortunately. attacks on humans became more common.

Recent Changes

In 1973, the Indian government realised that the tiger was endangered. Nature reserves were set aside where tigers could live safe from harm.

In China, the tiger was even more endangered. In 1949, there were about 4,000 Chinese tigers. Now, there are fewer than 50. In 1977, it became illegal to hunt tigers in China.

Poachers still hunt tigers, however, because they can still make a lot of money from making tiger medicines. Many farmers also hunt tigers living outside reserves. They worry that tigers may attack them or their animals.

Summary Of Arguments Against Tiger Hunting

1. Tigers are too rare to allow hunting to continue.

2. Medicines can be made using science and technology.

3. Tigers will only attack humans if they cannot find enough food.

Arguments For Tiger Hunting

Please read the following e-mail:

Dear Decision-maker:

I represent a group of villagers in northern India. We wish to be allowed to hunt tigers in our area for the following reasons.

1. Each family can only afford one or two animals, and we need them to give us milk and meat. Sometimes a tiger will attack and kill our animals. When that happens, it has very serious consequences for the family who owned the animals. Often, they cannot afford to buy another animal. A single tiger attack can ruin a whole family's livelihood for a long time.

2. Tigers still occasionally attack humans in our area. Because much of our farmland borders on the jungle where the tigers live, it can be dangerous to farm on this land. But there is nowhere else for us to live. If we cannot safely work on our land, we will not be able to feed our families. There will not be enough money or food to go round. Who is more important — a human or a tiger?

3. Many modern medicines, such as insulin for people with diabetes, are produced by using the organs of animals, such as pigs. If someone believes strongly that a medicine made from the organs of a tiger heals an illness, they should be allowed to use it. Even though modern science may not think that these medicines work, they might have some good effects. Only 20 years ago, most Western doctors thought that Chinese acupuncture was a waste of time. Now, thousands of doctors use acupuncture every day to help patients!

If there are enough tigers in zoos and reserves, why not allow us to protect ourselves from those that remain in the wild? We don't want to be attacked — would you?

Yours faithfully,
Concerned Farmers League

Back Forward Stop Refresh Home File Search Text Mail Online

Tigers: 123456

GO

You now have all the information required to make your decision. Remember, you must think about all the **facts** and **opinions** that you have read, and decide which ones you think are important. Once you have made your decision, you cannot change your mind. When you are ready, **make your choice**. Please proceed carefully.

ISSUE SHOULD **TIGER HUNTING** BE ALLOWED?

AGREE Click One **DISAGREE**

Tigers And Lions

Tigers and lions are very closely related. The two animals look similar except for the colour and length of their hair. However, their behaviour is very different. Tigers prefer to live alone, whereas lions like to live in groups, or 'prides'.

The two species are so closely related they can breed together. In some zoos, offspring have been produced. If the offspring has a lion as a father and a tiger as a mother, it is called a liger. If it has a tiger as a father and a lion as a mother, it is called a tigon.

Lions (pictured) are very closely related to tigers.

Endangered Cats

Many species of large cats are endangered, including tigers. Some are listed below:

Asiatic Lion: A kind of lion that lives in India, the Asiatic Lion is endangered because of human hunting and destruction of habitat.

Snow Leopard: Living in central Asia, the snow leopard is hunted for its fur.

Cheetah: Distributed between Africa and India, the cheetah has suffered from hunting and habitat loss.

Extra Facts: 3

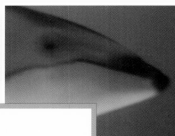

CITES

Most of the animals featured in this book are now protected by an international law called the Convention on International Trade in Endangered Species (CITES). In 1975, ten countries signed this law. Over the next 25 years, another 120 countries signed.

CITES makes it illegal for people to buy or sell parts of endangered species, such as their furs, tusks, horns or organs. It also bans the trade of live animals that are endangered. Together with other conservation activities, such as breeding in zoos and the establishment of nature reserves and national parks, people hope that endangered species will be protected, and will increase in numbers, for the future.

Summary

Bookweb Explorer

Thank you for your decision on tiger hunting. Your choice has been recorded, the Concerned Farmers League will be informed, and action will be taken.

You have now made decisions on the four conservation issues presented in this website. We know that this has not been an easy task, and we would like to thank you for reading the arguments for and against each important issue.

You may now understand that making these decisions is not as easy as you may have originally thought! Even with all the facts presented to you, you will have discovered that human emotion and human requirements are sometimes difficult to balance against the needs of the environment. If you wish to be involved in more decisions on the environment, your help and support would be welcomed on many issues. Thank you, and good luck!

QUIT

Index

Bookweb Links

Read more Bookweb 6 books about
endangered and extinct species:

A Wild Time! — Factual
Jurassic News — Fiction
Uncool! — Fiction
Whale Watch — Fiction

Key To Bookweb
Fact Boxes

☐ **Arts**

☐ **Health**

☐ **Science**

☐ SOSE

☐ **Technology**